MW01174073

Making Your Dreams a Reality

TAKING THE MYSTERY
OUT OF FINANCIAL PLANNING
NOT THE MAGIC—
ONE QUOTE AT A TIME!

Betty-Anne Howard, CFP®

With Maggie Ashton and Marlene Armstrong

ISBN-13: 978-1511543477
ISBN-10: 1511543477

Limits of Liability and Disclaimer of Warranty
The author and publisher shall not be liable for your misuse of this material. This book is strictly for informational and educational purposes.

Warning—Disclaimer
The purpose of this book is to educate and entertain. The author and/or publisher do not guarantee that anyone following these techniques, suggestions, tips, ideas, or strategies will become successful. The author and/or publisher shall have neither liability nor responsibility to anyone with respect to any loss or damage caused, or alleged to be caused, directly or indirectly by the information contained in this book.

Get Your Free Gift!

And Start
Making Your Dreams a Reality-
One Step at a Time!

With this free guide you will discover:

- What your dreams are made of.

- How your current situation can help create your road map.

- How to identify roadblocks along the way.

- How best to enjoy the journey.

- Identify the next small step you can take to make your dreams come true.

- And much, much more!

To get your free interactive guide to Start **Making Your Dreams a Reality**, go to www.bettyanne.net

Dedication

I would like to dedicate this book to my parents, Fred and Grace Howard, both of whom died too young and who still had the chance to teach me loads about life and what matters most.

Without even knowing it, they taught me many of the financial planning principles I use in my work including the one oftentimes ignored—that is, how to buck up and get back in the saddle when I fall, feel sorry for myself, or run out of energy. The message always was "we are called working class for a reason"!

My father, who couldn't read or write, taught me I could do whatever I set my mind to, regardless of any seen or unseen barriers I encountered—this from the man who was the secretary of his local union and whom no one knew was illiterate.

My mother taught me the importance, as a woman, to be self-sufficient and live my dreams, before getting married!

Given I was the only girl in a family of four boys, growing up poor, the biggest gift they gave me was knowing I was cherished. Thank goodness they didn't call me what they wanted to originally: Marvel-Anne!

Acknowledgments

The journey to making this book a reality has been one that spans a decade of pushing and pulling by others, and prodding and poking by many more.

I was told, "Don't lose your focus on your business by writing this book because you might just go bankrupt", "no one wants to have fun with money; this is a very serious business", "all that really matters is making money so how are you planning on doing that with this book?!", and so on—comments that scared me, threw me off my path, and made me seriously doubt, at times, who I thought I was and what the hell did I think I was doing?!

If it hadn't been for, the following people, this book wouldn't be here :

- The Kingston Writers Festival. I am always inspired by other authors.

- Trevor Strong, whose workshop I attended on writing humour at the Kingston Writers Festival and who, since that time, has given me so much more

- Wintergreen Studios and the writing workshops I attended with Helen Humphries (who encouraged me to explore fairy tales within my writing) and Lawrence Hill (who was the first person to suggest I find a way to make my business magical, for others)

- Unbridled Coaching, helping me move through my internal barriers to make this book a reality, with Marlene Armstrong and Maureen Donoghue

- Donna Kozik for her Write a Book in a Weekend and who inspired me to be more than I could have imagined, through my writing

- Eileen Chadnick, who suggested I take Donna's workshop and helped me realize this book was possible

- Brooke Warner and her Thought Leadership for Writers webinar series that got me thinking more about where I wanted to go as a Thought Leader within financial services, with my writing

- Kathy Sage, Minister Kingston Unitarian Fellowship and Christie Andrus kept me grounded in my values and always had an eye, ear & shoulder for me to lean on

- Jean Brereton, who reaffirmed that my life's purpose is to transform the financial services business (That's what she said!)

- Halla Tomasdottir, whom I just had to meet in Iceland when I read the article and saw her TED video on a feminine response to the financial crises

- Maria Nemeth, author of the *Energy of Money: Mastering Life's Energies,* who keeps telling me to just take that one small sweet step forward

- The MdDS support group on Facebook as we share our successes and failures, living with this rare form of vertigo

- My heart sister Heather, my brother Paul, and my best friend Julie, who all love me deeply, and believe in me, no matter what!

- Within my business we have a "Dealer," which I always found ironic given I worked in addictions for years and never had one of those then. Here I am now, working in the money business, with one! Investment Planning Council has done something remarkable in that they've embraced who I am in this business and encouraged me to be the unique soul that I am rather than trying to rein me in. Quite remarkable.

- Finally, I have to dare greatly and acknowledge the woman of my dreams, Maggie Ashton, who has singlehandedly made so many of my own dreams a reality. She is the best life partner and soul mate a woman could have.

A portion of the proceeds from the sale of this book will be used for creative and artistic projects related to Money and Financial Planning.

Praise for This Book

"Become enchantingly inspired as you read this delightful yet meaty quote book. As Betty-Anne transparently shares her humble beginnings and weaves her personal story throughout, you will feel warmed and inspired, and trust this author in her infinite grassroots wisdom about being knocked down, brushing yourself off, and reaching your goals with your money. The feel-good life lessons and quotes make for an enjoyable read that truly motivates the reader to get smartly involved with her money."

Kathi McKnight
Denver, Colorado
Speaker, Author, Master Graphologist
Author, *Explore Your Core:*
Unlock the Magic the Write Way

"Horses, magic, unicorns, phoenix rising! What, you may ask, does this have to do with financial planning? Read on my friend as Betty-Anne Howard has managed to tap into the heart and soul of our industry with the help of her co-creators.

This book is a rare gift: motivating, inspiring, while

educating you about the true nature and what is at the core, for many of us, working within financial services."

Chris S. Reynolds
Toronto, Ontario
President and CEO,
Investment Planning Counsel Inc.

"Betty-Anne Howard and her co-contributors take the mystery and 'chore' out of financial planning and infuse it with fun, meaning, and a big dose of inspiration. Laid out is a lovely spread of quotes, ideas, and personal anecdotes that bring financial planning alive. This isn't a 'money' book. Rather it's a testament to the integral relationship between financial planning with life—and fulfilling one's life dreams and aspirations.

While Betty-Anne brings tremendous credibility to financial planning as an experienced CFP (Certified Financial Planner) professional, what makes this book stand out is her voice. Infused with wonder, awe, clarity, and a big dollop of fun, this book is full of heart and soul."

Eileen Chadnick, PCC, ACPC, ABC
Toronto, Ontario
Author, *Ease: Manage Overwhelm in
Times of "Crazy Busy"*
Principal, Big Cheese Coaching

"Betty-Anne has a truly unique method of having people think about money and its value in their life from the heart and soul perspective and she's captured it in this user-friendly, reflective resource.

She has a way of making the often-intimidating world of finance accessible to those who want to create the life they really dream about.

You've come to the right place if you are yearning to thoughtfully connect your use of resources to what really matters in your life today and for all those tomorrows."

Christie Andrus, MA
Kingston, Ontario
The Human Factor

"What I love and appreciate about Betty-Anne's book is each chapter is joyfully serious.

A scene is painted and a provocative question asked.

I was left both thoughtful and inspired.

And, I should also add, I was left seriously joyful!"

Tim McElvaine
British Columbia, Canada
President, McElvaine Investment Management Ltd.

"What a delightfully unique book! I was hooked right from the start.

Think about it: dreams, quotes, and financial planning all together in the same book?

Turns out it is not only an interesting combination, but also a useful one.

Reading this book invited me to slow down and take the time to look into my own heart and wake up, dust off, and explore possibilities that I hadn't thought about in years.

Betty-Anne's combination of wonderful quotes, simple exploration, personal examples, and to the point questions is magic. *Making Your Dreams a Reality* invites you to participate rather than just passively read, it is a call to clarity, and sweet action. It is a bridge between your dreams and reality. A bridge I highly recommend crossing."

Lori Savage
Los Angeles, California
Coach, Executive producer, *The Energy of Money*

"Little did we know when we moved to Ontario from Alberta nearly twenty years ago that Betty-Anne would become an integral part of our lives.

Initially, she and Kevin worked together for an employee assistance firm, helping people deal with their problems.

When she became a financial planner we decided it was time to move our investments to her since our trust in her was already established. We quickly came to discover that investments were only a small portion of the services we have enjoyed from Betty-Anne and her team at Making Dreams a Reality Financial Services.

She has become an advisor and mentor to us and our adult children, who now have their own growing families. As educators we understand the importance of encouraging our children to plan for their futures and are grateful that Betty-Anne helps that happen.

This book will be an excellent resource and tool for any individuals or families who want to embrace the meaning behind the money while making the world a better place to live."

Rebecca Luce-Kapler, PhD
Associate Dean, Graduate Studies and Research
Faculty of Education, Queen's University at Kingston

"If there is a formula for financial success, I believe that Betty-Anne Howard along with Maggie Ashton and Marlene Armstrong have cracked it. It's not enough to inhale endless stats and facts about how to create and make the most out of money. There are endless books that do that.

Making Your Dreams a Reality asks the questions that must be asked if one is to truly succeed and yet does it with such charm, inventiveness, and humour that the reader becomes the learner without really knowing how that happened. That's true alchemy! A must read if you really want to succeed."

Monica Parker
Inspirational Speaker and Actress/Producer
Author, *Getting Waisted: A Survival Guide to Being Fat in a Society That Loves Thin* and *OMG!: How Children See God* (coming Christmas 2015)

"Betty-Anne and her co-writers have done a tremendous job at interweaving valuable quotes and life lessons followed by guidance in helping us to seek out their application in questioning our own set of financial values.

As a parent, teacher, and award-winning children's book author, I enjoyed this quick read and reflection on life and how by questioning our beliefs, thoughts and goals—we can help plan for and shape our financial future."

Jeanette Ramnarine
Belleville, Ontario, Canada
Mom, Teacher, and Award-Winning Author, *The 4 Little Pigs* (a financial values book for children)

"I loved this book. As a professional in the financial industry who has been involved with clients and money for over 30 years, I was eager to read the next page and ponder. I know it could help my clients and friends and others take the steps to make their own personal dreams, a bright and vivid reality.

It is possible to create your plan. Learn how to set your goals, for your future and move your dreams to your new reality while achieving your full potential.

Give yourself a gift.

Take the time to read this book, knowing it will make you smile at times, pause at others, and truly think what matters most to you. With the clarity that comes with each chapter, you can focus on who you are now and who you might become.

Betty-Anne has presented a wonderful book that guides you to invest in yourself and get results."

Kathryn A. Wright, CFP, EPC, CDFA, CPCA, CFDS
Certified Financial Planner, Elder Planning Counsellor, Certified Professional Consultant on Aging, Chartered Financial Divorce Specialist
Wright Wealth Strategies Inc.,
Kingston, Ontario, Canada
A financial services professional who has been around clients and money since 1980.

"Betty-Anne and co-contributors have created a life manual in this clear-to-read book.

The steps outlined are designed to show readers how to fulfill their dreams. These best life practices are highlighted in a financial narrative but underscore best behaviours for a full sum life.

The clear-to-read approach provides the motivation for readers of all levels to gain the teachings within this life manual.

Because Betty-Anne's life's work is to achieve and help others achieve dreams, this book will be a blessing for every reader to better living.

Enjoy."

Omari Whyte
Regional Vice President,
Investment Planning Counsel
Mississauga, Ontario, Canada

"Your book reminded me of so many people that I have met in my life and career who are controlled and emotionally 'owned' by finances.

For many fascinating reasons, some of which are ingrained in our DNA, trouble understanding money, how it works, what it is and isn't is for, plagues us.

While money cannot buy you happiness, it also isn't the root of all evil.

There is some powerful wit and wisdom in this book that shines some light in the corners, and reminds us all what it is to be financially independent."

Dennis Mosley-Williams
DMW Strategic Consulting, Ottawa, Ontario, Canada
Author, *Serious Shift: How Experience Delivery Can Save Your Practice* (2013)

"Similar to how Susan Cain's *Quiet* revolutionized the way the world views introversion, this deeply insightful book promises to revolutionize the way we all view another frequently misunderstood subject: the field of financial planning.

Howard offers an examination of a topic that takes up much of our time—money—and somehow manages to do so in such a fresh, charming, and inviting manner that even the most finance-phobic out there will find themselves won over.

Overflowing with inspiring quotes and illuminating anecdotes, this is a book for anyone seeking clarity regarding their personal finances—that is to say, everyone."

Brooke Warner
Publisher, She Writes Press
Berkeley, California

"So many of us are focused on the future: thinking, wishing, planning for it.

Betty-Anne drills down to the core of why financial planning is so much more than numbers and projections for the future. As she puts it, 'Infusing the meaning behind the money' creates an environment where the seemingly contradicting aspects of living for today and planning for tomorrow become harmonious.

She reminds us that money is a tool—a tool that can be used to help realize our dreams and the dreams of those we love NOW and in the future.

This is mandatory reading for my family! Bravo, Betty-Anne!"

Dan Nolan, CFP, CIM, FCSI
IPC Securities Corporation
Nepean, Deep River and Kingston, Ontario, Canada

"This is not your typical financial planning book. It is much more than that; it's about life planning.

Making Your Dreams a Reality is an innovative and fun way to look at *why* we are investing.

Through her experiences and insights, Betty-Anne has developed an interesting way to get the reader to reflect on their dreams and potential ways to achieve them.

There will be obstacles along the way, but with the help of a financial planner, you can create a road map that could help you live your dreams."

Brian Lavoie, CFA
Vice President, Sales,
Northwest Ethical Investments, Canada

"I read Betty-Anne Howard's book during a time when I was moving through great transition; the timing of synchronicity always surprises me!

Her quotes, interpretations, and calls to action really inspired me to reflect upon what my next move was going to be during my personal and business evolution. I always have so many ideas going on in my head at the same time that I can become chaotic and lose track of my intentions.

Making Your Dreams a Reality is an impactful tool for us all as we mindfully focus on what we want to accomplish, financially and otherwise.

As an Authenticity Coach, I find that most of us lose sight about who we are and how we want to show up within our goal setting. Betty-Anne supports us in bringing our souls to the forefront before even thinking about the money piece of what we want to accomplish.

This book is a lovely blend and balance of personal development and financial planning."

Diana Reyers
Authenticity Coach
CEO, Daringly Mindful™ Coaching
Facilitator, Trainer, and Community Builder,
Authentic Leadership Global™
Vancouver, British Columbia

"This book is warm, heartfelt, and most of all inspiring. It captures the true essence and importance of financial planning in a fun, thought-provoking way.

Grab a cup of tea, sit down, and enjoy! Betty-Anne's candour is refreshing and will leave you wanting more."

Sarita Rebelo, MPA
Wife, Mother, Policy Analyst,
and Client of Betty-Anne's
Ottawa, Ontario

"Betty-Anne Howard has been a constant supporter and promoter of local independent business and financial literacy in our community. Betty-Anne is more than words; she is change in the making.

Shortly after moving to our community she gave of

herself with a swim-the-lake fundraiser for community improvements, which was a huge success, raising thousands of dollars.

Betty-Anne is an inspiration. I trust you will find her book inspiring and thought provoking."

Terri Dawson
Owner, The Green Gecko
Lyndhurst, Ontario (where Betty-Anne lives,
population 250)

"Betty-Anne has taken the normally dry and sometimes 'scary' subject of financial planning and created a resource full of personality and personal insight. The book's format is the first thing you notice, with each gem of wisdom headed by an appropriate quote, but don't let this fool you. Betty-Anne's own journey and wisdom in each section show a pathway that will give understanding as to the importance of financial planning, and the personal story and anecdotes make this a great read that is both educational and entertaining.

With practical lessons on financial stability and life lessons throughout, this book really shows that professional financial planners are approachable, too, and have experiences just like our own on their journey through this life. I recommend this book highly to anyone wanting to further their financial success."

Ian Campbell
ADV Dip Multimedia, Cert TAA, Australia
Web designer, Teacher, Multimedia Expert,
and Entrepreneur

"*Making Your Dreams a Reality* takes you on a journey that re-ignites the dreamer in you, inspires you to see what is possible instead of what is and deepens your commitment to your future.

It offers not only the road map but the resources to leap the road blocks and reminds us that the magic is in the journey. One quote a day, one action a week, and your life will be changed."

Debora J. McLaughlin
Nashua, New Hampshire
Author, *Running in High Heels: How to Lead with Influence, Impact & Ingenuity*
CEO, The Renegade Leader Coaching &
Consulting Group

"Betty-Anne is a woman of her word; she said she would find a way to communication how to have fun with money and she has. *Making Your Dreams a Reality* has accomplished just this.

Let Betty-Anne's personal and professional journey take you on a ride of self-awareness, reflection, and goal-setting all the while bringing a smile to your face. You won't even know you are planning for your financial future. Ready or not, this is an incredible voyage worth embarking on."

Jodie Harrison
Regional Vice President, TD Asset Management
Ottawa Ontario

"I first met Betty-Anne five years ago at a conference through Advocis, our professional association, in Toronto and we got along like a house on fire.

Betty Anne is not just a financial planner. She is a life coach and has written a motivational book that inspires people to live their truth and then teaches them how to carve out a financial path that aligns with their core values."

Jackie Porter, CFP
Writer and Speaker
Carte Wealth Management
Toronto, Ontario

"Congrats on your book, Betty-Anne, Maggie, and Marlene!

It's splendid—refreshing and relevant. A reminder of everyday gifts and the extraordinary potential we all have.

Thank you for sharing your gifts and weaving together an exquisite reflection of life and lessons."

Rebecca Darling
Senior Business Consultant
Small Business Development Centre
Kingston Economic Development Corporation
Kingston, Ontario

"Betty-Anne's book is full of sparkling jewels based on her life, insights, love of horses, financial wisdom, and much more. She delights and amazes, helping us see the path for making our own dreams a reality."

Toni Erickson,
Boulder, Colorado
Psychotherapist and Relationship Coach

Contents

About the Author and Co-Creators

B etty-Anne Howard, Maggie Ashton, and Marlene Armstrong spent an entire weekend, between meals and riding horses, and gathering with friends, discussing the meaning behind these quotes, going deeper both personally and professionally.

Betty-Anne Howard has a unique background for someone in financial services.

Before becoming a Certified Financial Planner®, she spent 17 years in the social and emotional health services field as a counsellor and teacher. This experience, in addition to her Master's Degree in Social Work and Honours Degree in Psychology, has informed her more holistic approach to Financial Planning.

For her, Financial Planning isn't just about the money; it's about "the meaning behind the money."

Betty-Anne is passionate about making information accessible to all and is driven to connect and educate.

During her time helping to set up alcohol and drug referral centres throughout Eastern Ontario in the 1980s and 1990s she co-wrote and was first editor of *Alcohol and Drug Problems: A Practical Guide for Counsellors*, a textbook that addressed gaps in training, and that remains a popular text in colleges and universities today.

In her current role as a financial planner, she has written many works, including "What Women Want" an article in *Advisor's Edge* based on the innovative work she did in combining her background as a training consultant and financial planner.

Her blog, "Making Your Dreams a Reality," tackles financial issues, one at time, in a clear and playful manner. And her story "Breathe Out, Breathe In, Write, Observe, Sit" appears in *Writing at Wintergreen: An Edited Anthology by Helen Humphreys.*

A financial planner for 17 years, Betty-Anne, helps her clients by treating financial planning as a natural extension of life planning. She strives to make her writing and conversations interesting, relevant, and—here's a word you don't hear often in financial planning—fun.

Maggie Ashton is a tax specialist who has a heart and soul that yearns to help people understand our very complex and frustrating tax system. www.ashtontax.ca

Marlene Armstrong is the President and CEO of

Foxview Stables Inc. (www.foxviewstables.com) and a certified Equus Coach at Unbridled Coaching (www.unbridledcoaching.com), partnering with horses, not riding them, to powerfully move you through your barriers in realizing your dreams.

Foreword

by Trevor Strong

This is not your ordinary book about financial planning.

And that's because Betty-Anne is not your ordinary financial planner.

After all, before she was a financial planner she was a teacher and a social worker. Oh, and she also worked in a prison. And you thought financial planners were boring!

I first met Betty-Anne at Kingston Writersfest. She was attending the humour-writing workshop I was giving and came up afterward to tell me that she wanted to write a personal finance book that was interesting, relevant, and, above all, fun! She asked me what I thought, and I told her it sounded like a great idea—little did I know that I would be helping her write that very book!

That book, *Making Your Dreams a Reality: A Stress-Free Guide to Take the Mystery out of Financial Planning, but Not the Magic!*, is coming out soon, by the way—a sequel, if you will, to the book you have in your hands right now.

But back to the book at hand.

You are in for a treat. Why? Because soon you will be rid of the uneasy feeling you get when you think about your personal finances.

I know the feeling, and it comes from fear—from bad habits formed in childhood, from the endless stream of incomprehensible financial acronyms that bombard you, from that all-pervasive message you get from newspapers, finance shows, and the media, telling you that if you don't get your finances in order—*right now!*—you'll spend your golden years in a cardboard box under a bridge fighting rats for scraps of garbage.

It's no wonder so many people put off financial planning. After all, what do we do when we're scared? Scurry into a corner and hide or spend money!

Hide no more! Come out and look around. See, things aren't so bad after all!

This book doesn't tell you what to do. Instead it asks what *you* would like to do. It is an invitation, not an order.

Breathe a little, take your time, and discover how to make money work in your life and how to make your dreams a reality, one quote at a time.

Trevor Strong
Author, Songwriter, Humorist
Kingston, Ontario

Foreword

by Maria Nemeth, PhD, NCC

It is very rare to meet someone in the financial field who has the ability to encounter her clients the way Betty-Anne Howard does.

This book is about creating your money life in a way that reflects your true values, vision, and dreams. Having consulted in the financial field for more than 20 years I've seen brilliant formulas and strategies for crafting financial plans. However, this book will encourage you to take a gentle look, deep within to discover and then act upon your most important life goals.

It is no secret that how we do money is how we do our lives; money finds its way into every aspect of living from our vocation, relationships, health, recreation, and the contributions we want to make to our community. This book will serve as a thoughtful guide. Read it slowly, and take time to consider the quotes and the questions that Betty-Anne poses.

You'll find a new sense of freedom and lightness. After all, our relationship with money does not have to be adversarial, but one of friendship, connection, and support.

Maria Nemeth, PhD, NCC

Founder and Director, Academy for Coaching Excellence

Author of the Best-Selling Books *The Energy of Money* and *Mastering Life's Energies*

Voted One of the UK's 50 Most Influential in Financial Services

Singing in the Silo

A book of haiku, tanka, and haibun

Philomene Kocher

www.SingingInTheSilo.ca/

so long ago
when others overheard me
singing in the silo
something dormant inside me
is ready to sing again

Chapter 1

Dreams

Our dreams propel us forward,
compelling us to come up with a plan to take us there!

||||||||||||||||||||||||||||||||||||||||||||||||||||||||||||||||||||||||||||||||||||

1. "Nothing happens unless first a dream!"
~ Carl Sandburg

See it, create it, believe it!

Your dreams can come true if you breathe air into them, convincing them to come alive!

Follow your beliefs, regardless of what other people think or believe. You can make your dreams a reality.

As a child, I dreamed of having a horse. Back then it was a status symbol; you needed money to own a horse. Now I have two.

A Few Questions for You: What are your dreams? What were your dreams? How can you bring them back to life so you can build the foundation you need to make them a reality?

||||||||||||||||||||||||||||||||||||||||||||||||||||||||||||||||||||||||||||||||||||

2. "You see things and say, Why?
But I dream things that never were and I say, Why
NOT!"
*~ **George Bernard Shaw***

How can you make the impossible possible? By bringing your dreams into creation, imagining what doesn't yet exist. Do you have the ability to see what is not yet there? Can you become a believer in the unseen, the unknown?

I was the first person in my family to go to university. My father couldn't read or write. We were poor. I dreamed of being a teacher because I wanted someone to listen to me, believing I had something important to say.

Something for You to Consider: How have your beliefs inspired your dreams? How can you ignite your sense of possibility?

||||||||||||||||||||||||||||||||||||||||||||||||||||||||||||||||||||||||||||||||||||

3. "What one loves in childhood stays
in the heart forever."
*~ **Mary Jo Putney***

What touches your heart in childhood—the magic of horses, unicorns, Pegasus, puppies, kittens—can fill your heart with enduring unconditional love.

Children's minds are open with a sense of wonder and tenderness—free spirited. The seeds planted in childhood with cultivation will bloom, even as an adult.

I loved to read as a child, even biblical things like Joseph and his coat of many colours and Daniel in the lion's den.

A Question for You: What stirred your heart as a child? How can you touch what's at your core while bursting at the seams with passion for your life today and in the future?

||||||||||||||||||||||||||||||||||||||||||||||||||||||||||||||||||||||||||||||||||||||||

4. "We welcome passion, for the mind is briefly let off duty."
~ Mignon McLaughlin

Passion is the fire that burns away doubts and fears. The warmth soothes our bones.

Passion allows you to dream and takes away the negative thoughts pervading our minds, at times.

Our minds are always at work; our passion washes that away, bringing clarity, bringing hope or faith.

I was determined to go to university, collecting pop bottles along the side of the road, cleaning houses, selling paint and wallpaper—whatever it took, I was going to do it and I saved almost every penny I earned.

Something for You to Consider: In what ways does your passion fuel your greatest desires, and how can your money keep that fire burning?

〜〜〜〜〜〜〜〜〜〜〜〜〜〜〜〜〜〜〜〜〜〜〜〜〜〜〜〜〜〜〜〜〜

5. "Dreams come in all shapes and sizes.
What are your dreams made of?"
~ Betty-Anne Howard

None of your dreams are more or less important.

Individuality, diversity, and uniqueness all make sense when working with your dreams.

We live in a society that, at times, suggests that bigger is always better—homes, cars, vacations. This view squelches the very real notion that *more* doesn't mean happier or more satisfied with life.

I remember when I came into the business of financial planning and I was told that at some point I would want to buy a car that reflected my success, like a Mercedes or a Lincoln. I drive a Fiat 500, as this car is in alignment with my values of being both frugal and an environmentalist.

Something for You to Consider: What are a few of your favourite things? And why?

‖‖

6. "A dream doesn't become a goal until it is written."
~ Edwin Louis Cole

I once asked a woman who came to see me what her dreams were.

She looked at me as though I'd asked her to eat an elephant! She had no idea what I was asking of her. Dreams were faded memories for a single mother working hard all her life, about to retire.

Now, at 72, she gets excited to share her dreams with me. We write them down and talk about what she needs to make them a reality.

She sits with them, meditates, prays for additional guidance from her higher powers, then we can make decisions together for that one next sweet step to be taken.

A Few Questions for You: When was the last time you wrote your dreams down and came up with the plan to make them a reality?

‖‖

7. "You are never too old to set another goal
or to dream a new dream."
~ C.S. Lewis

I often get asked why, at the age of 58, I decided to start riding horses and taking dressage lessons.

Horses have always been there, beckoning me to come to them, and finally the universe gave me the proverbial kick in the butt and I landed at Unbridled Coaching because I'd read an article in the newspaper about their offerings.

This, I thought, *is something I've always been interested in doing,* so off I went.

The rest is history!

Something for You to Consider: What of your dreams are still there, and remain to be realized and fulfilled?

||||||||||||||||||||||||||||||||||||||||||||||||||||||||||||||||||||||||||||||||||||||||||||||

8. *"A goal is a dream with a deadline."*
~ Napoleon Hill

Taking our dreams and turning them into goals that are SMART is a process. I am a process junky!

Trusting the process, being in the moment, and dreaming can go hand in hand with setting **S**pecific, **M**easurable, **A**chievable, and **R**ealistic goals.

The **T** is for Time frame—setting a deadline, which means saying out loud and writing down when you want to get there. It may not happen, and even if it doesn't you can adjust your time frame if you have to.

A Question for You: Can you start with one dream followed by a SMART Goal and write it down?

||||||||||||||||||||||||||||||||||||||||||||||||||||||||||||||||||||||||||||||||||||||||||||||||||||||||||

9. "Indeed—judicious, consistent parenting is a dream of mine. No judgments, learning space, and listening carefully are my goals."
~ Emma Thompson

Making your and my dreams a reality is a dream of mine.

Creating a financial plan within an environment that allows for both living for today while taking steps to plan for the future are my goals.

Infusing the meaning behind the money into this process is also my goal.

Whenever someone comes to me with an inheritance I ask if they would like to think about and plan what they will do with this money based on whom it came from and what was important to that person so we can bring that energy into our plans for their future.

Something for You to Consider: If you were to give some thought to the energy of money, where might that take you?

‖‖

10. "There are a lot of people who have dreams, goals, and hopes, but there aren't a lot who get to see them realized."
~ Tyler Perry

There are many people around the world who dream of clean water, a place to go to the bathroom, a roof over their heads, warmth, and safety.

We should never lose sight of our privileges while others are suffering, even in our own backyards.

As a feminist, from years gone by, I am painfully aware of who has power and privileges in our world, which sometimes comes as a big surprise to most people when they hear what I do for a living.

What we do with the money we make and how we spend it can make a difference in other people's lives.

A Question for You: Have you considered how you could make money while making a difference in other people's lives?

‖‖

11. "When we are motivated by goals that have deep meaning, by dreams that need completion, by true love that needs expressing, then we truly live."
~ Greg Anderson

I feel so blessed to, with the help of others, have made so many of my own dreams a reality: living on a lake, owning and riding a horse, and running a profitable business that is uniquely mine.

I have many more dreams I hope to complete, including writing this book and another one, and then another one.

Education has always been a key to unlock so much of where I want to go with what I have in my life. I admire those who can write well, using words to take me to a place I've never been before, articulating my thoughts and feelings.

Underneath all of this is a foundation of love that is essential for me to succeed, and this includes self-love, an ongoing and rewarding process.

Something for You to Consider: How have you infused meaning and love into your dreams?

Chapter 2
Road Map

There are many different roads that can take us to our destination. Your guiding principles will determine the look and feel of yours.

||||||||||||||||||||||||||||||||||||||||||||||||||||||||||||||||||||||||||||||||||||||||||

*1. "Do not go where the path may lead;
go instead to where there is no path and leave a trail."*
~ Ralph Waldo Emerson

Take a moment so I can speak to the importance of following your heart, embarking on a journey of self-discovery. And yes, both your heart and mind are companions on your journey to making your dreams a reality.

You need to create and follow your own path, just as I do mine. Success isn't always intentional; it's the creativity that gets you there.

I needed an outlet for my creativity, so I began writing with Trevor Strong, humorist, song writer, and entertainer, about money and financial planning.

A Question for You: How can you be a leader, a trail-blazer, in your own life?

||||||||||||||||||||||||||||||||||||||||||||||||||||||||||||||||||||||||||||||||

2. "The most difficult thing is the decision to act;
the rest is merely tenacity."
~ Amelia Earhart

It takes courage to come to a decision that you are going to embark on that trip, knowing that you are choosing the path that is right for you. It takes endurance at times, and there's no going back once you make the decision.

Like cantering a horse, once your leg shifts back ever so slightly, you are in it!

You can go back from a canter to a trot or a walk. Each requires a different stance. All are important to learn. It takes tenacity, perseverance, and practice.

On my road to becoming a teacher, when I graduated from university I was told there were no jobs, I went back to waitressing so I could make some money while waiting for things to change, looking for different opportunities, and biding my time, until I could teach.

A Few Questions for You: What will you need in order to make that decision to act? At what speed and cadence? How will you remain tenacious?

||||||||||||||||||||||||||||||||||||||||||||||||||||||||||||||||||||||||||||||||||

3. "Without story, information is nothing but
a load of bricks lying about waiting for someone to make
constructive use of them."
*~ **Aidan Chambers***

Creating a plan requires your story, the meaning behind the money, the energy it holds for you. Story is the mortar that holds the bricks together; the bricks symbolize the information. Together they construct the image, the vessel to take you on your journey.

Your individuality and uniqueness come through your story. They provide you with the significance.

Story is the starting point. Creating a plan can get you to a different ending.

My story begins in a small village with three older brothers who weren't that much older than me, eating venison because that put food on our table, and was part of my journey to becoming a vegetarian. One year during hunting season all my father shot was a bear.

Something for You to Consider: How does your story differ from others? In what ways does it help or hinder you on your path to making your dreams a reality?

II

4. *"Look where you are going and you might just find yourself there!"*
~ *Wendy Waller*

Financial planning is looking ahead, looking up where you are headed, and becoming aware of your destination.

On a horse, if you look down, on the ground, you could end up there.

When riding you try your best to always look where you are going, with your eyes directed ahead, trusting and knowing that is what the horse needs, to get you there.

I had no idea how powerful horses could be in teaching me lessons about how I show up in the world and challenging me to keep trying, never giving up.

One step at a time, small goals, small bites, looking ahead, mindful of where you are going.

A Few Questions for You: What is that one next small sweet step you can take to get you one step closer to making your dreams a reality? Can you see where you are going?

||||||||||||||||||||||||||||||||||||||||||||||||||||||||||||||||||||||||||||||||||||

5. "The best thing about the future is that
it only comes one day at a time."
*~ **Abraham Lincoln***

Taking it one step at a time, one day at a time, and sometimes one moment at a time, what's the alternative? Living in the past? The future? Neither will get you where you want to go.

It's the tenacity—the momentum from each day—that can propel you forward.

Each day, in my business, I try to focus on what I need to do that day, in that moment trusting that I can make my dreams a reality.

Something for You to Consider: What are you going to do today, in this moment, to make your dreams a reality? What is your next baby step?

||||||||||||||||||||||||||||||||||||||||||||||||||||||||||||||||||||||||||||||||||||

6. "If you're doing your best, you won't have any time to
worry about failure."
*~ **H. Jackson Brown, Jr.***

If you are doing your best, there is no failure. We all make mistakes and there is important learning from those mistakes.

There are no mistakes, only retakes. Like in the movies or on TV shows, even the bloopers can sometimes be the best part.

Financial planning takes time and energy, and at times you will fall down. A plan will include contingencies—what to do when you encounter a hurdle along the way.

I have had many setbacks in my personal life and in my business. Each time the temptation is to say, "What's wrong with me? Why don't I get it?" After I've licked my wounds I stand back up, get back in the saddle, and ride.

Something for You to Consider: How have you done your best, especially when you've encountered a hurdle in your path, along your way? How does it feel to get back in the saddle?

—————————————————————————

7. "Education is what remains after one has forgotten what one has learned in school."
~ Albert Einstein

Street smarts are as valuable as formal education.

Living life is an education from which we blaze our trail to making our dreams a reality.

Life teaches us many valuable lessons we take with us on our journey.

I have always valued education—both types: formal and life learning.

My desire to never feel that shame again because of the shack I lived in as a child, the roast bologna with cloves and mustard sauce for Sunday dinner, the desperately out-of-style, hand-me-down clothes given to me by my older cousins, propelled me to learn more about how money works and how I could plan so that I wouldn't ever have to experience those things again.

A Question for You: What are your most valuable lessons in life that continue to beckon you, speaking your name, asking you to do it this way (or, that way!)?

||||||||||||||||||||||||||||||||||||||||||||||||||||||||||||||||||||||||||||||||||

8. *"There are only two mistakes one can make along the road to truth: not going all the way, and not starting."*
~ *Buddha*

What will it take to get you started on the road to making your dreams a reality? How might you be challenged to go all the way?

During the financial crises of 2008–2009 I almost didn't go all the way.

I was thrown off my path so badly I needed a lot of support to get back in the saddle and ride. Limping with the weight of watching the stock markets go down, and down even more, I was in a state of shock, wishing I had seen it coming (no one did!) so I could have done something. I wasn't worried about my own investments because I knew the markets would come back up, and they did; they usually do. Thank goodness for planning ahead with cash buffers and cash wedge strategy; that's what made the difference in all our lives, during that trying time.

Something for You to Consider: How have your challenges thrown you off your path or made you stronger? How have you gotten back in the saddle and continued to ride?

||||||||||||||||||||||||||||||||||||||||||||||||||||||||||||||||||||||||||||||||||||||||||

9. "A good financial plan is a road map that shows us exactly how the choices we make today will affect our future."
~ Alexa Von Tobel

I so often hear this very same question posed in different ways. It always comes down to finding that delicate balance between living for today **while** planning for the future. Not an easy pose to hold.

Having said that, the two are intricately woven together, and sadly too many of us don't seem to get that!

Buying a horse may mean I have to postpone my

retirement for a few more years. Buying a second horse?! Hell yes! Had I considered volunteering at a horse ranch so I could ride for free? Absolutely.

A Question for You: How will your choices today affect your future?

---

10. "A person often meets his destiny on the road he took to avoid it."
~ Jean de La Fontaine

My journey through life has had multiple twists and turns, even though I mapped it out clearly, for myself.

The problem is that in life we will, for better or worse, share our lives with others who have their own path to follow. The intersection points can be gentle and soothing, and at other times a minor minefield. Most of us would choose to avoid even minor explosions, and yet chaos seems to be with you, wherever you go.

We all have our lessons to learn in life, finding ourselves back in familiar situations while asking, *Haven't I been here before?*

Something for You to Consider: In what ways has your destiny unfolded, even when you tried using avoidance? Isn't it interesting how the same lessons are delivered in different ways until we get it?

||||||||||||||||||||||||||||||||||||||||||||||||||||||||||||||||||||||||||||||||||||

11. "The high road is always respected. Honesty and integrity are always rewarded."
~ *Scott Hamilton*

How often have you regarded an unhappy customer as a gift? Same goes for someone who totally disagrees with your hypothesis that working with a financial planner who wants to have some fun is an aspiration worth pursuing.

Taking the high road—using emotional intelligence while speaking your truth—isn't always easy and is necessary. No less a balancing act than any other.

Living with my own conscience. I am the one I must go to bed with each night.

A Question for You: When have you had to take the high road, no matter how difficult that was, and how did your integrity and honesty remain intact?

Chapter 3
Roadblocks

Roadblocks are the inevitable detours, stop signs,
and bumps in the road along the way.
Throughout your journey in life,
as you encounter these,
don't give up! Get back in the saddle and ride.

<hr>

"Hardships often prepare ordinary people
for an extraordinary destiny."
~ C.S. Lewis

Isn't this the truth! We all have hardships to varying degrees, and that's what makes us stronger and builds character, fortitude, and resilience.

We are all ordinary people with the ability to do something extraordinary with our lives.

When you hit rock bottom, there's nowhere else to go but up. A resilient spirit will bring you to becoming the Phoenix rising.

When the markets were tanking in 2008 and 2009

I was terrified! I didn't really bother to care about my own investments for my retirement. As the steward of other people's money I felt I should have known better—that somehow this financial crisis was my fault. I learned that there are things I don't have any control over while reminding myself that I am a planner, and that's something I can do: plan!

A Question for You: How might you benefit from the hardships in your life, turning lemons into lemonade?

‖‖

2. "The difficult is what takes a little time,
the impossible takes a little longer."
~ Fridtjof Nansen

The impossible, or so it may seem, is in fact possible. Everything is possible.

Speaks to tenacity and never giving up.

Can you see yourself looking down the rabbit hole? It's dark and yet full of possibilities.

Gives you hope and faith. Hold on—it will happen. Everything is possible.

Back to the financial crises of 2008–2009, I finally understood why in 1929 some people jumped off buildings. The same thing happened during this crisis. I reminded myself that I was a planner and we would now need to sort out what impact this crisis had on our children's education, our retirement, and our lives, and adjust our plan accordingly.

A Question for You: How have you experienced the impossible only to find it is possible?

||||||||||||||||||||||||||||||||||||||||||||||||||||||||||||||||||||||||||||||||||||||||||||

3. "I can forgive, but I cannot forget, is only another way of saying, I will not forgive. Forgiveness ought to be like a cancelled note—torn in two, and burned up, so that it never can be shown against one."
~ Henry Ward Beecher

If you can forgive and don't forget, are you really forgiving?

You are actually forgiving yourself, your piece in what happened. In some ways people blame themselves, based on their story. In order to move forward in your life, forgive yourself first.

There is a lot of shame that goes with money. You can become overwhelmed, feeling defeated and despair. Your confidence can become lost. A learning can come from forgiveness.

Horses forgive almost instantly, and only remember trauma when it is triggered. They live in the present moment, they don't think about the past or the future.

I had to look beyond my father's alcoholism to see his strengths—how he didn't let a little thing like not knowing how to read or write stand in his way of being the secretary for the local chapter of his union. My mother was a trained stenographer, and she helped him. I have forgiven my father while acknowledging the great gifts he gave me: strength, perseverance, and obstinacy.

Something for You to Consider: How can you live for today while planning for the future? How might you need to forgive yourself and perhaps others in order to move on with your dreams?

||||||||||||||||||||||||||||||||||||||||||||||||||||||||||||||||||||||||||||||||||||||||||

4. "Obstacles are those frightful things that you see when you take your eyes off your goal."
~ Henry Ford

We will always hit roadblocks in our lives. They are inevitable, and that is often ignored by many people.

The key is to see them as a fact of life. Don't let them derail you, and try to plan for them as best you can.

Sometimes when we ride our horses they see dragons where there are none. It is our job as the rider to reassure them they are not there. Comforting, reassuring and persevering. Keeping our balance when they jump sideways to avoid the dragon.

A Few Questions for You: How might the obstacles you've encountered stood in the way of taking you where you would like to go. Who is there to comfort and reassure you?

||||||||||||||||||||||||||||||||||||||||||||||||||||||||||||||||||||||||||||||||||||||||||||

5. "I don't fix problems;
I fix my thinking then problems fix themselves."
~ Louise Hay

Our attitude or mindset, when we encounter road-blocks, is a key factor in how well we deal with them.

If you are handed lemons, are you able to make lem-onade?

I have had many bad experiences throughout my life, so I am constantly working on my thinking, my mindset, my deceptive brain messages—challenging myself to change the stories I tell myself about my own success and money.

Something for You to Consider: How have you turned a bad experience around? How has your thinking impeded your ability to make your dreams a reality, and how can you turn those stressful and often untrue thoughts around?

||||||||||||||||||||||||||||||||||||||||||||||||||||||||||||||||||||||||||||||||||||||||||

6. "Optimist: someone who figures that taking a step backward after taking a step forward is not a disaster. It's more like a cha-cha."
~ Author Unknown

I picked up this quote in the Facebook universe and sent it back out for comments amongst my friends. Here is what they had to say:

"Turn up the music! It's all a dance." ~ Monica Parker

"This quote helps both the advisor and the client to keep their attention on their goals, not their setbacks." ~ Patricia Thatcher

"This is a fantastic quote, Betty-Anne! It's true about financial planning and it's true about life." ~ Jackie Porter (who is also a financial planner)

"Just back from Cuba, so it's feeling more like a salsa!" ~ Shirley Bailey

"As a dance enthusiast, I love this quote. Yes, it relates to financial planning. My immediate thought was when you see some of your investments slide back a bit, don't worry; they will bounce back in time (if you got a good financial plan or planner). Create a good plan and be optimistic about it for the long haul." -Jean Haley Folsom

"You win some, you lose some. Enjoy the dance! Pretty much how money works." ~ Patricia Drury Sidman

"Haha. This is so true in money and in life. It's all about the dance and how much you enjoy the dance. If you are optimistic, the dance is fun, like the cha-cha. I agree with Jean Haley Folsom: Create a good plan with your financial planner and you have every reason to be optimistic about your money and your life…." ~ Marlene Armstrong

I love to dance and plan. The working title for this book was "Let's Have Fun With Money™: Come Dance with Me and I'll Show you How." Financial planning is very much like a dance: I teach you the steps, and we create the dance.

A Question for You: How does optimism play a role in your life?

||||||||||||||||||||||||||||||||||||||||||||||||||||||||||||||||||||||||||||||||||||||

7. "It is a rough road that leads to the heights of greatness."
~ Lucius Annaeus Seneca

Do you have any idea the number of times I've relied on quotes such as these, to keep me going, motivated, alive?!

"When the going gets tough, the tough get going" was also a favourite of mine. It became a mantra—my badge of honour.

The message always was and still is: no pain, no gain!

While I see the merits of this approach I have now reached a place and time in my life where I want to revel in the greatness, be in the moment, and leave my struggles behind. Stand on top of them triumphantly and say, *I did it!*

Something for You to Consider: How have the rough moments in your life led you to greater outcomes?

||||||||||||||||||||||||||||||||||||||||||||||||||||||||||||||||||||||||||||||||||||||

8. "Failures, repeated failures, are finger posts on the road to achievement. One fails forward toward success."
~ C.S. Lewis

Risking failure is never easy.

According to Dennis Moseley-Williams in his book

Serious Shift: How Experience Delivery Can Save Your Practice, "the only unique competitive advantage is the exceptional experience an advisor can create for his or her clients."

A very tall order. And a very good book, I might add.

A tall order that at its very core means taking risks, trying different things, finding out what works. And, of course, what works for one won't necessarily work for another.

That's the fun in the process, along with listening, hearing, sharing stories, understanding.

A Question for You: How might you risk failure for the sake of succeeding?

---

9. "All you need is the plan, the road map,
and the courage to press on to your destination."
*~ **Earl Nightingale***

I don't know who Earl Nightingale is, but I sure know who Florence Nightingale was.

The image that gets conjured up for me is a woman who felt such passion about her calling, shining her flame in a burning lantern on the road to improving health care. A courageous woman called on to go down a path that others had not yet found.

I don't know if she had a road map. Maybe not—perhaps it was all intuitive, something she felt deep in her heart, a knowing that this was the right thing to do.

I had to learn more about Earl Nightingale and this is what I found, when I Googled him:

> "best remembered for the recording that he wrote and narrated in 1956, called, The Strangest Secret. In his profound message he tells us that, 'we become what we think about', and then, he spent the rest of his life, giving us examples of how this is true, and how to use this universal law to direct our lives in the most productive ways we can."

How fitting!

Something for You to Consider: Dare greatly and call on courage to pursue your dreams and come up with a plan.

‖‖

10. "I spent a lot of years on the road, and what happens is you find out who your real friends are and you find out where your strengths and weaknesses lie in communication. I've had the same friends for 20 years now and I can count them on one hand."
~ Sarah McLachlan

Friends, like humour, are great companions on our life's journey.

I have half a handful of friends whom I've known for over 30 years. They are my guideposts, my pillars, my "prop me up when I fall," "we believe in you and what you are trying to do" kind of friends.

I have new friends, too.

Developed through the horse community as well as Bass Lake and Lyndhurst cronies. They encourage and support me, and are there with an ear to listen or a shoulder to catch my tears.

A Few Questions for You: How do you decide who will remain as your friend? What role do your true friends play in your life? In your financial plan?

11. *"Determination gives you the resolve to keep going in spite of the roadblocks that lay before you."*
~ Denis Waitley

Determination, combined with your vision of where you want to go and who you want to be, can take you places you might never have dreamed.

I was determined to become a teacher. What happened along the way was 18 years ago. I'd gone above and beyond all of my greatest expectations, in my life and career.

What's next? I asked myself and my financial planner.

Lise Allin suggested I consider coming into this business, financial services. "We need people like you," she said.

The learning curve was very steep, steeper than I could have imagined. And, I am back working on going above and beyond my greatest and wildest expectations.

Something for You to Consider: How might your determination be needed when encountering roadblocks along the way?

Chapter 4
Are We There Yet?

***The magic is in the journey itself.
That's half the fun of getting there!***

|||||||||||||||||||||||||||||||||||||||||||||||||||||||||||||||||||||||||||||||||||||||

*1. "As my mind can conceive of more good,
the barriers and blocks dissolve.
My life becomes full of miracles popping out of the blue."*
~ Louise Hay

As we remain open and welcoming to limitless possibilities, the universe works with us to provide.

When you see positive things, the roadblocks disappear.

I remember once being filled with fear regarding a big life change. My fear was this enormous brick wall that dissolved when I turned back to look at it, from the other side.

A Few Questions for You: Do you believe in miracles? If you had a magic wand and you were financially successful, what would your life look like? How would you feel? What would you be doing?

||||||||||||||||||||||||||||||||||||||||||||||||||||||||||||||||||||||||||||||||||||||

2. "To me magic is those unexpected surprises and serendipitous moments which seem to appear... sometimes asked for, sometimes not...to delight and amaze us."
~ Toni Erickson

Living life to its fullest can surprise and amaze us.

In so many ways, it really is the little things that matter most, creating meaning and purpose in our lives—all the things that money actually can't buy:

a shared spontaneous laugh with a loved one, hearing a baby gurgle and coo, watching a puppy play, supporting your friend or mother who is finished her chemo treatments and is going to live!

Something for You to Consider: What delights and amazes you in your life? How much of that requires money?

||||||||||||||||||||||||||||||||||||||||||||||||||||||||||||||||||||||||||||||||||

3. "Magic to me is the unknown force I wonder will
appear for my writers and me, if invited, always does."
~ **Donna Kozik**

After experiencing the Write a Book in a Weekend®
course with Donna Kozik, I came to realize that she
does exactly what I do, as a financial planner.

She creates an environment where learning and
success can happen, using a variety of tools and techniques: coaching, creating, motivating, and inspiring us
with her years of experience.

This learning process helped bring one of my many
dreams into reality and inspired me to dream even
more.

*A **Question for You:** What tools and support do you
need to bring more magic into your life?

||||||||||||||||||||||||||||||||||||||||||||||||||||||||||||||||||||||||||||||||||

4. "Isn't it interesting how we never really see ourselves
as successful until someone else
recognizes the success in us?"
~ **Melissa Rowe**

We so often look outside of ourselves for validation,
thus rarely seeing our own success.

This is so often true, for women especially. It has
been true for me.

Financial planning offers an opportunity to see your situation through our eyes. This process can be revealing; sometimes you are richer than you think.

Horses mirror back to you how you show up in the world, a very powerful experience. Horses are great coaches, helping you move forward to be a better leader and work through your barriers, just like a financial planner, a money coach, who mirrors back to you how you show up with your money.

Something for You to Consider: How do you show up in the world? How have others recognized the success in you? How have you recognized your successes?

||||||||||||||||||||||||||||||||||||||||||||||||||||||||||||||||||||||||||||||||||||||||

5. "The larger the island of knowledge, the longer the shoreline of wonder."
~ Ralph W. Sockman

The more knowledge you have, the more possibilities.

Knowledge can come from experience.

The more I learn, the more I want to explore and discover about life, relationships, and matters of the heart. The joy is in the learning.

Knowledge opens up the world that is full of wonder, vitality, creativity!

Those who share their knowledge help others to

learn and grow, empowering you to make informed decisions, and giving you more choices and options in your life.

A Question for You: What else do you need to know at this juncture in your life to feel empowered, able to move forward with making your dreams a reality?

||||||||||||||||||||||||||||||||||||||||||||||||||||||||||||||||||||||||||||||||||||

6. *"Energy is the currency of the universe. When you 'pay' attention to something, you buy that experience. So when you allow your consciousness to focus on someone or something that annoys you, it reciprocates the experience of being annoyed. Be selective in your focus because your attention feeds the energy of it and keeps it alive. Not just within you, but in the collective consciousness as well."*
~ Emily Maroutian

What you focus on, transpires. In other words, or in the language of financial planning, money is energy, and if you focus on the 'lack' of money, you will attract more 'lack.' Focus instead on gratitude for what money has already brought to you and you will get more of that.

I feel very privileged in my life to be able to buy new clothes and organic vegetables, supporting local businesses.

I try to write in my journal every day the 10 things I

am most grateful for and the five things I accomplished that day, focusing my attention on what I did get done and not the thousands of things I didn't—exiting from the mindset of overwhelm to one of clarity, focus, ease, and grace (Dr. Maria Nemeth, *The Energy of Money*).

A Question for You: How can you shift your focus to one that includes clarity, focus, ease, and grace?

||||||||||||||||||||||||||||||||||||||||||||||||||||||||||||||||||||||||||||

7. *"It's a long old road, but I know I'm gonna find the end."*
~ *Bessie Smith*

Oh boy! Do you know where the end is? My answer: I certainly don't! Is there even an end?

How do you celebrate your accomplishments? Enjoying that precious moment when you've either taken the giant leap off your cliff of doubts and fears only to find yourself soaring?

Or, landed on your feet, happy to have survived?

Something for You to Consider: Do you ever become overwhelmed with your journey, the road you are on, the path you are following? How could you find a way to make the road ahead enjoyable and fun?

‖‖

8. "Map out your future—but do it in pencil. The road ahead is as long as you make it. Make it worth the trip."
~ Jon Bon Jovi

The moment you have a plan in place, it changes. Why, you ask?

Because that's the very nature of life and living it. Things change, if not today or tomorrow, sometime in your near future.

You may lose a job or a loved one and, then, that changes everything. Except the foundation of what you've already built.

Shannon Moroney wrote a brilliant book about forgiveness, *Through the Glass,* a story of going to hell and back when her husband committed horrific violent crimes and knew that instant that the life she had known was destroyed. She once said to me, "No one plans for your life being turned upside down and, we need to, because it can happen, to anyone."

Something for You to Consider: Why might a pencil be a more valuable tool than a pen, when coming up with your roadmap for the future?

||||||||||||||||||||||||||||||||||||||||||||||||||||||||||||||||||||||||||||||||

9. "If you don't like the road you're walking,
start paving another one."
~ Dolly Parton

"Easier said than done" might be your response.

We can all get stuck on the path we're currently on.

Staying open to the other possibilities is one thing. Starting to pave a whole new path requires work, significant energy and time, on your part.

A Question for You: How might you access some other workers for the paving job ahead of you?

||||||||||||||||||||||||||||||||||||||||||||||||||||||||||||||||||||||||||||||||

10. "Life isn't about finding yourself. Life is about
creating yourself."
~ George Bernard Shaw

Finding yourself was always a bit of a joke in my circles, of psychologists and social workers! Why, you ask?

Because we understood that life wasn't about finding yourself like some prize in the Cracker Jack box.

Life quite clearly was and continues to be about your day-to-day experiences that start to define who you are.

A Question for You: How have you created yourself and what have you created?

‖‖‖

11. "We do not remember days; we remember moments."
~ Cesare Pavese

Does it seem like a contradiction to hear a financial planner talk about being, and staying, in the moment?

I cherish the precious moments with my family, my friends, my loved ones, my horses.

I also feel particularly blessed these days because I am cherished back.

Life goes by so quickly. Why wouldn't I want you to stay in the moment? Be present in your my life?

Something for You to Consider: What do you remember about your most precious moments?

Chapter 5
Tools of the Trade

In order to make our dreams a reality
we need a blueprint and tools.

Important to keep in mind:
To a hammer, everything looks like a nail.

||||||||||||||||||||||||||||||||||||||||||||||||||||||||||||||||||||||||||||||||||||||

1. "The safe way to double your money is to fold it over
once and put it in your pocket."
~ Frank Hubbard

Investments are a means to making your dreams a reality. Most do require some capital.

Too often we are lured into believing that investment returns, like doubling our money, will get us there quicker, which is true—if it were possible. My experience has shown me that the amount of risk you could potentially take is not worth this, as a possibility, over a short time period.

A much better way to double your money is to not spend so much of it.

Marlene - I always saw savings as: *no point!* I associated saving with denying myself something; my savings are now my cushion, giving me peace of mind, a sense of safety, an accomplishment. Something I can tap into when I need it the most. Changes your whole energy about money.

I saved almost all of the money I made when I was young, out of fear. Obtaining an education was my ticket to freedom, or so I thought, and I wanted to be sure I had sufficient funds to get myself there because my parents weren't in a place where they could help me financially.

A Question for You: How might you keep more money in your pocket, spending less and saving more?

||||||||||||||||||||||||||||||||||||||||||||||||||||||||||||||||||||||||||||||||||||||||||||

2. "Financial planning is very similar to learning how to ride a horse. We bring the tools and they bring the blueprint."
~ Betty-Anne Howard and Mark Rashad

Weighing in at 1,200 pounds, a horse is a powerful animal who is in tune with their environment and you. If you are upset, tired, or anxious, they will reflect this back to you. Imagine an anxious or upset 1,200-pound animal under you!

When learning to ride, being mindful of your position—what you do with your hands, legs, eyes, and body, along with your emotional state are the tools we bring to the experience and the horse's nature—is the blueprint.

The missing ingredient in this picture is the riding instructor who can carefully and skillfully combine all of these components, allowing learning to ride a horse to occur.

A financial planner is a lot like a riding instructor or coach, in that you bring your emotions, history, story, and attitude, while we bring the knowledge and tools to help you craft your own financial plan or blueprint for your life.

Before I started working with a financial planner, a quarter of a century ago, way before I came into this business, I had no idea what a financial planner actually did. I knew what I didn't want. Someone telling me what to do with my money or selling me something I didn't want—that was my fear. My financial planner, Lise Allin, who eventually brought me into this business, taught me a lot about money and how to get the most out of it. More importantly, she earned my respect and for that I am extremely grateful.

Something for You to Consider: What has your blueprint looked like thus far? What are the additional tools you need to help build the life you desire?

||||||||||||||||||||||||||||||||||||||||||||||||||||||||||||||||||||||||||||||||||

3. *"Change requires intent and effort."*
~ Roxanne Gay

Tools are one thing; your mindset is quite another. When they work together in tandem you stand a much better chance of getting to your destinations in life.

Intention means willingness to change, and sometimes stress and pain combine to create that intention.

Horses reflect back to you your true intention. You can go into an arena with a horse and if what you are saying is not your true intention, and if deep down inside, something very different is going on that perhaps you don't want to face, they'll smoke that out of you without judgment.

In financial planning, I can be seen as a saviour, and the reality is only you can save yourself.

You are the one who needs to work your plan. I can provide the tools, guidance, and support; I am here as your coach and your guide. Just like the horse is your coach and guide—to keep you moving forward. And, it's a partnership. I can't want this more than you; it's your work that needs to be done.

Something for You to Consider: Tell me what changes you think will require intent and effort. Take a mirror and look closely. Tell me what you see.

‖‖

4. "The average pencil is seven inches long, with just a half-inch eraser—in case you thought optimism was dead."
~ Robert Brault

This reminds me of the importance of keeping it simple. Pencils were once a tool; now we have spreadsheets.

You can erase with a pencil; that doesn't make it a mistake. There are no mistakes—only retakes!

How we perceive the tools and what we do with them are equally important. To a hammer, everything looks like a nail.

Cash flow and net worth are tools used in financial planning. One is to measure where the money will come from, to make your dreams a reality, the other to measure how it's going.

What money is coming in, what money is going out, and where is it going are excellent starting points. You can use a pencil to track this. Similarly, what you own versus what you owe is a measure of your net worth. Write it down, calculate it, and then use this information to measure how you are doing, year over year.

I used to think that the simplicity of this meant it had no value. Now I track it religiously, personally and for my business. I do the same for the people I work with and their businesses. I insist on it.

A Few Questions for You: What would your cash flow and net worth say about you? How might you take this information and use it as a tool to make your dreams a reality?

|||||||||||||||||||||||||||||||||||||||||||||||||||||||||||||||||||||||||||||||||||

5. *"Money is a tool to bring my dreams to life. It is a substance that I have the power to create more of."*
~ *Doretta Gadson*

There are many different ways to bring the power of money into our lives without giving it too much power.

Serving people is a higher intention and if we trust in that process, the power of that can bring us more money. At the same time, being of service and making a profit can be mutually inclusive, even though as women we often struggle with this concept. We can make a decent wage and be of service.

Money is one of the tools that helps to bring our dreams to life, and simplicity in our lives determines how much money we need.

A Question for You: What role does money need to play in your life to bring your dreams alive?

||||||||||||||||||||||||||||||||||||||||||||||||||||||||||||||||||||||||||||||||||||||||||||

6. "How can a society that exists on instant mashed potatoes, packaged cake mixes, frozen dinners, and instant cameras teach patience to its young?"
~ Paul Sweeney

We live in a society of instant gratification. If we want something we give it to ourselves regardless of the consequences or outcomes. More debt, anyone?

Patience is not only a virtue, it is a necessary ingredient—part of our mindset tools.

At the same time, you can make instantaneous decisions, trusting your intuition that can have positive long-term consequences. Frozen dinners can provide us with sustenance, if that's all you have in your freezer and there's nothing else to eat. A packaged cake mix can mean the difference between a birthday cake for a child and family, on a limited budget, and no cake.

A packaged cake mix takes me back to being a child. Kraft dinner is a treat—simple and easy, although not very nutritious, especially if I eat it with ketchup.

A Question for You: How do you strike that delicate balance between living for today while planning for the future?

‖‖‖

7. "Striving for excellence motivates you; striving for perfection is demoralizing."
*~ **Harriet Braiker***

Our attitude is one of the many tools we use in making our dreams a reality. Perfection is an illusion.

If you have an attitude of doing the best you can, then you'll achieve your goals.

Think of parenting—we recognize that our parents did the best that they could with the knowledge they had at the time.

Psychotherapy, Equus Coaching, and financial planning can take you from good to great—from being well to fantastic!

I have done all three, at different points in my life, as I continue to strive to take that great leap and live in my zone of genius (Gay Hendricks) while staying open to the art of possibility (Roseamund Stone Zander and Benjamin Zander).

A Question for You: How has your financial plan helped you to move toward being your fantastic self?

||||||||||||||||||||||||||||||||||||||||||||||||||||||||||||||||||||||||||||||||||||||||

8. "The difference between perseverance and obstinacy is that one comes from a strong will, and the other from a strong won't."
*~ **Henry Ward Beecher***

Financial planning is an organic process, like planting seeds, growing and developing with the sun, water, and tender loving care.

How you come into this process is reflected in your attitude and willingness to see your life through my lens. Patience adds to your perseverance and keeps you open to possibilities. A growth mindset—your building blocks!

Being obstinate is the opposite of a growth mindset; it is a fixed mindset, being closed to the possibilities. It takes time to build your plan and for it to grow. It's organic, and if you get off the path, you have to find a way to get back on.

I had a plan: Get an education, teach, buy a starter house, pay down debt, and buy my dream home, on a lake. Ten years ago my plans got blown out of the water! It almost shattered my faith in planning as I questioned: How could this have happened, to me?! This major setback only served to make me stronger, fitter, and more determined than ever to keep pursuing my dreams.

A Question for You: How have you become stronger as a result of your life's challenges? How have you persevered?

||||||||||||||||||||||||||||||||||||||||||||||||||||||||||||||||||||||||||||||||||||||||||||||

9. *"A great accomplishment shouldn't be the end of the road, just the starting point for the next leap forward."*
~ ***Harvey Mackak***

A great accomplishment could be:

1. Graduating from college or university and the question then would be: *Now what!? What am I going to do with my education? What type of career do I want and who might hire me? How much money do I want or need to make?*

2. Getting married could mean: *When can we afford to buy a house and how many children do we want to bring into this world?*

3. Buying your first house could mean: *How do I ensure I have the money should I need to replace the old furnace, buy some new furniture, or paint?*

4. Reaching your retirement could mean: *How do I want to spend my "go-go" years and my "slow-go" years?*

5. Knowing that you are going to die someday and you ask yourself, *How might I want to leave a legacy?*

Something for You to Consider: Once you've accomplished your next goal, what will your next leap forward be?

॥॥॥

10. "Standing in the middle of the road is very dangerous; you get knocked down by the traffic from both sides."
*~ **Margaret Thatcher***

Politically I have never shared any of Margaret Thatcher's views, yet I recognize she was a force to reckon with.

She wreaked havoc on Britain's working class, and was hated and revered by many.

I remember being challenged by Karen Armstrong, the force behind the Charter for Compassion.

She was the one who asked that we listen to others whose opinion is the opposite of our own, solely for the purpose of thinking differently about a situation—an approach she believes can lead to better communication and the changes in our world we so desperately need.

A Question for You: How might an alternate world view change how you see your own?

<hr>

11. "A person has to remember that the road to success is always under construction. You have to get that through your head. That it is not easy becoming successful."
~ Steve Harvey

And with that construction, depending on the stage you're in, your road to success requires very different tools, trucks, equipment.

It helps if you work on developing a growth mindset, one where you embrace challenges, see effort as a path to mastery, learn from criticism, and find lessons and inspiration in the success of others.

With a growth mindset, according to Carol Dweck, you can reach ever-higher levels of achievement, which gives you a greater sense of free will.

A Question for You: When was the last time your road to success was under construction?

Chapter 6
How to Have Some Fun
Along the Way

Humour, at times, is a very nice companion to have
on your journey to success!

‖‖‖

1. "There is little success where there is little laughter."
~ Andrew Carnegie

If you don't have fun and laughter in your life then there really is no success. We can infuse our success with joy and laughter.

A part of this includes not taking ourselves so seriously, enjoying our lives with a touch of laughter.

You can be happy in your core without money, but if you have money and you aren't happy, is that success?

I work in a very serious business, dealing with millions of dollars, helping people make enormous decisions in their lives that will also impact generations to come. At a particular point I decided I either had to find a way to bring my creativity into the financial planning process with my clients or I didn't want to do this anymore. I now work with Trevor Strong, who has a master's degree in education. Humour was the topic of his thesis—how to bring humour into the classroom. That's what we are doing and trying to figure out: how best to bring humour into the financial planning process, staying open to the possibilities.

A Question for You: How do you bring laughter into the success of your life?

꜒꜒

2. "Humour is the affectionate communication of insight."
~ Leo Rogfsten

Insight, or your a-ha moments, often bring you laughter—as in, "how silly of me" and then you giggle.

When I think of laughter, I think of being joyous. When I link insight with joy, it comes down to feelings of inspiration, passion, and being in the moment. Pure creativity.

Sometimes I need to use humour to get people to loosen up, so they can talk freely and easily about the difficult things in life, like dying, or becoming disabled or critically ill. Or, what would happen if the two of you split up? It's important to talk about this now and not when your ex has run off with their lover.

A Question for You: When have you been able to laugh at yourself? How did that help you move forward with insight?

||||||||||||||||||||||||||||||||||||||||||||||||||||||||||||||||||||||||||||||||||||||||||

*3. "The best thing about the future is that it only comes,
one day at a time."*
~ Abraham Lincoln

Did you smile when you read this quote? Can you relate to it at all?

We assume that planning is about the future—and it is. However, it is even more about what you do today.

Don't let planning become this big monster, like thinking about your own mortality; let it bring you into the present moment while planning for the future.

Taking it one day at a time became the mantra for Alcoholics Anonymous. Sometimes all we can do, for now, is take it one day at a time.

Horses live in the present moment; they worry not about the past nor the future. That is probably why they are so grounded and help bring us to a place of peace.

What's this got to do with having fun along the way,

you ask? Sometimes fun is simply a smile you put on your face when you know you've done a good job for today, while recognizing that tomorrow is another day.

A Question for You: How can you put a smile on your face, today, right now, in this moment?

<hr />

4. "Laughter is the shortest distance between two people."
~ Victor Borge

Financial planning can be intimidating—scary at times—and many people put it off because of that.

Sharing a laugh should be an integral part of this process, as it helps us to lighten up and, when appropriate, take a breather from the planning, share an experience that relates, and add a bit of fun.

Nervous laughter also tells me when someone is uncomfortable; I need to take more time, be more sensitive, and explore the meaning behind the laughter.

A Question for You: How has laughter helped shorten the distance between you and someone else?

||||||||||||||||||||||||||||||||||||||||||||||||||||||||||||||||||||||||||||||||||||

5. "Anyone who takes himself too seriously always runs the risk of looking ridiculous; anyone who can consistently laugh at himself does not."
~ Vaclav Havel

This makes me think of *Improvisation of the Spirit,* a book written by Katie Goodman: **"The skills required for improvisation are the skills needed for any collaborative or creative process: stay present, be flexible, let go of the goal, gag your inner critic, listen to others with an open mind, don't struggle, give and take, trust yourself and the process, and more."**

I laugh a lot when I ride my horse, especially when I am in a lesson. Wendy Waller, my riding instructor, tells me this is a good thing because it helps me to relax and, should I fall, my body will hurt (hopefully) a little less when I hit the ground relaxed.

We often punish ourselves when we should be celebrating our challenges—our falls in life—as gifts, given to us by the Universe while teaching us a thing or two.

A Question for You: When are you able to laugh at yourself?

‖‖‖

6. *"Humor is the great thing, the saving thing. The minute it crops up, all our irritation and resentments slip away, and a sunny spirit takes their place."*
~ Mark Twain

Planning for the future is no mean art, and for its sake you must live for today.

Each side of the same coin is necessary for the coin to exist.

Humour and seriousness are different sides of the same coin.

Having fun with money is the humour part, enjoying what your money can buy while injecting some pleasure and fun into the saving and investing part.

My concern is always that if we're not having fun doing this—planning for our future—then why do we bother? Seeking some pleasure through the process will mean we want to do more of it.

Something for You to Consider: How can you have more fun with money, by saving and investing it?

‖‖‖

7. *"Good humor isn't a trait of character, however. It is*

an art, which requires practice."
~ David Seabury

I remember attending a conference on Isa Mujeres and meeting Monica Parker, who had me in stitches, practically rolling onto the floor with laughter.

I left there with two things: Monica as my friend and a very strong desire to bring the funny back into my life.

It is true: Humour is not a word that one often finds in my business. However, Monica stirred something inside me, a deep knowing that humour is an essential and yet tremendously missing element in my business.

I went searching and found others who agreed. #Fun With Money was shown the light of day, & her brightness still needs to be polished and shone.

A Question for You: How has humour played a significant role in your life?

8. *"A person without a sense of humour is like a wagon without springs. It's jolted by every pebble on the road."*
~ Henry Ward Bleecher

How often have you heard "smile" or "come on—don't you even have a sense of humour?" These words are veiled commands to do what someone else wants.

I am happy to say this is not what I am talking about here, when I think of having a sense of humour.

Humour is much more complex than these commands from another. It is much more subtle; the nuances can be like a dance, delicately choreographed by you with another. It's much too important to be reduced to telling someone to smile!

Something for You to Consider: How has humour given you springs in your wagon?

|||||||||||||||||||||||||||||||||||||||||||||||||||||||||||||||||||||||||||||||||||||||||||

9. "I have survivor skills. Some of that is superficial—what I present to people outwardly—but what makes people resilient is the ability to find humour and irony in situations that would otherwise overpower you."
~ Amy Tan

I remember taking a writing weekend workshop with Lawrence Hill, author of the now highly regarded novel *The Book of Negroes*. We were to send him a situation that was powerful, moving, memorable, and yet difficult.

I wrote about my experience choking down bear meat, because that was what my father had shot during hunting season. We were reminded that we were lucky to have food on our table. It was a horrible experience for me.

You aren't going to believe what Lawrence asked me to do: Rewrite it, he said, with a sense of humour. I thought he had lost his mind, especially given I wrestled with that idea almost daily. How could I? How could anyone possibly find anything humorous about that experience?

It took me a while and I finally did it, appreciating the task he'd assigned to me.

A Question for You: How might you be able to inject a little humour into the things that have pained you?

|||||||||||||||||||||||||||||||||||||||||||||||||||||||||||||||||||||||||||||||||||||||||||

10. "There's no life without humour. It can make the wonderful moments of life truly glorious, and it can make tragic moments bearable."
~ Rufus Wainwright

I can look back on my life now and smile where there used to be fear and unhappiness, sometimes even disgust, when I think of the tragedy I endured, not just as a child but as an adult, too.

I have learned from the mistresses and masters of humour—the ones who have truly made me laugh, in a wholesome, kind, yet piercing way.

The ability to make me laugh during those wonderful moments and while sharing my painful experiences is a precious gift.

Same goes for the work I do. If we can have some fun along the way, it doesn't get much better than this, or does it?

Something for You to Consider: How has humour made your life brighter, richer, happier?

⁙⁙

11. "Mixing humour and harsh reality is a very human behaviour, it's the way people stay sane in their daily lives."
~ Jorge Garcia

I used to work in the psychology department at the Prison for Women, which once was the only federal prison for female offenders in Canada.

What does that mean, exactly?

I worked with women who had murdered others (sometimes this was their second time around), women who were heroin addicts and told me stories about men with guns coming to get them, to pay their debts, women who were abused in the 35 of the 37 foster homes they'd lived in, and aboriginal women who were denied their families, their history, their traditions, their lives.

We used humour to cope, all of us, as we ate our

lunch in the psychology department.

A Question for You: How do you use humour to cope?

Chapter 7
The World in Which We Live

Answering the "why" of our business tells you a lot about who I am and what's important to me, within the context of the world in which we live.

<hr>

1. "Try not to become a man of success, but rather try to become a man of value."
~ Albert Einstein

This speaks to a higher intention/purpose within your business. Money is a byproduct.

What's most important are your values and the higher purpose of your business or what you do.

Not just doing a job for the sake of it. How do you measure success? In many ways, including understanding your purpose. Seeing your value in the purpose of the job.

Becoming a person that you value—your "why." Serving others in your own way.

Something for You to Consider: Do you understand your "why"? Why you do what you do, for money?

How have you incorporated your own values into this?

---

2. "No one can whistle a symphony. It takes a whole orchestra to play it."
~ H.E. Luccock

It takes a village to raise a child.

You are not alone!

Teamwork is vital, and you can't do it alone—even though you sometimes think you can. Realize you are not alone and there are people who are happy to help you.

I often reach out to friends, colleagues, colleagues who have become friends, and other loved ones in my life when I need a helping hand, and I am not afraid to ask, although sometimes I wait too long to do so.

A Question for You: How can you seek help at this juncture in your life and from whom?

---

3. "The most vital businesses rise above the technicalities of their operations to engage people in a clear conversation about what matters most in life and the enterprise of making their way in the world."

~ *Keith Hanna*

Stepping back from the mechanics of cash flow, investments, and net worth, and quantifying your goals to understand the human side—the analysis of the human factor.

Coming to understand the story, the conversation about why, and how we can help.

At Unbridled Coaching, the mechanics are cleaning the stables, getting the hay, feeding the horses, and giving them water. The conversation is "What would you like to work on?", "Where are you feeling stuck?", "What are you ridiculously good at?" so you can think about and act on the splendour of you.

At Ashton Tax, in tax preparation there are the bio-mechanics of the tax return itself—the numbers. The conversation is about understanding who the person is: What are your hurdles? What are your challenges? What keeps you awake at night?

Something for You to Consider: What does keep you awake at night and why?

||||||||||||||||||||||||||||||||||||||||||||||||||||||||||||||||||||||||||||||||||||||||||||||||

4. "One life is all we have and we live it as we believe in living it. But to sacrifice what you are to live without belief, that is a fate more terrible than dying."
~ Joan of Arc

Gives me goose bumps when I think about it.

Living a life with beliefs and values keeps you alive with passion and purpose. It addresses the core of answering the question of why we do what we do.

Within financial services the assumption at times is that we're greedy, thinking only of ourselves, when, for many of us, that is far from the truth.

A Question for You: How have you integrated your beliefs and values into your life and financial plan?

||||||||||||||||||||||||||||||||||||||||||||||||||||||||||||||||||||||||||||||||||||||||||||||||

5. "Just making money is ultimately a boring job—making money and making a difference is interesting. You are pursuing a higher purpose and reaping a more fulfilling kind of profit that entails."
~ Keith Hanna

Ultimately this is what financial planning is all about—making a difference in people's lives.

Building trust, building relationships, and being there when I am needed are the goals.

We all need to do what we can to run a profitable business so our business is sustainable; monetary profits are one thing. It's what we put into our jobs, how we benefit from serving others—a higher purpose—that profits us greatly.

Something for You to Consider: How do you make money and make a difference?

||||||||||||||||||||||||||||||||||||||||||||||||||||||||||||||||||||||||||||||||||||||||||||||||

6. *"Every man is a damn fool for at least five minutes every day; wisdom consists in not exceeding the limit."*
~ Elbert Hubbard

No one is perfect. We need to recognize and embrace our own imperfections.

Like the gambler, we need to know when to hold them, and know when to fold them.

You need to take calculated risks at times—we all do—and we need to know when to pull back from those risks. Knowing your limits—that is true wisdom.

Helps if you can laugh at yourself, when you are a damn fool!

A Question for You: When was the last time you were a damn fool?

||||||||||||||||||||||||||||||||||||||||||||||||||||||||||||||||||||||||||||||||

7. "Work needs to be a reflection of your social values.
You are how you work!"
~ Leigh Steinberg

The UN Principles for Responsible Investing include social responsibility.

What that means to me is that companies are treating their employees well, interacting responsibly with their community, and adhering to the "profits with principles" philosophy. I first heard that phrase when a client of mine shared Halla Tomasdottir's TED video with me. Her talk has had almost 500,000 views; it's reached a lot of people. She talks eloquently about managing money with feminine principles, and that includes emotional capital. People, she says, run companies, not spreadsheets.

Halla shook my world. I wondered how she allowed herself to say what I have thought so often, out loud, to so many people. I knew I had to meet her.

I was treated like royalty when I arrived in Iceland to meet Halla, coming to know and understand what made this woman tick and how she arrived at this place.

Something for You to Consider: How are your values reflected in your work?

||||||||||||||||||||||||||||||||||||||||||||||||||||||||||||||||||||||||||||||||

*8. "I'm saved every day by the intrinsic value of the work
I do, which I truly enjoy."*
~ Al Jarreau

I love hearing "You have made my dreams a reality!"
There's nothing more satisfying than that.

Financial planners across Canada right now are
a threatened species. If we are to go the route of the
United States and the United Kingdom, then financial
advice will only be available for those who have money,
like so many other things in life.

I find this disturbing and upsetting, and my professional association, ADVOCIS, is trying to do everything within its power to keep financial advice available
to all Canadians.

Something for You to Consider: How aware are you of
the financial advice landscape, our designations, and
what they mean? How we get paid and for what services?

||||||||||||||||||||||||||||||||||||||||||||||||||||||||||||||||||||||||||||||||

*9. "The quality of your work, in the long run, is the
deciding factor on how much your services are valued by
the world."*
~ Orison Swett Marden

What I have found in the 17 years I've worked in this

business—migrating from social work and teaching to financial services—is that not all financial planners/ advisors are created equal. Some do only want to sell you something so they can make money from you and then move on to the next sell!

I have also found that we are either loved or hated.

Many of us are loved by our clients, who appreciate all that we do for them and their families, even going so far as to say, "I don't know what we'll do without you."

We are hated by others who question our motives, our reasons for being in this business, our credibility, and our practices. Apparently we are loathed almost as much as lawyers, in some circles.

I go to bed at night knowing I've made a difference in someone's life. I've helped ensure they will have a great retirement and their kids will go to university without any of the worries I had about money.

Knowing that I have helped someone protect what they've worked for all their lives from a disgruntled partner they are now leaving.

And, knowing that both I and they will leave a legacy for children, grandchildren, or the work that will go on when we die, to make the world a better place to live.

Something for You to Consider: What has been your

experience with a financial planner? Did you feel they were working in your best interest?

〰〰〰〰〰〰〰〰〰〰〰〰〰〰〰〰〰〰〰〰〰

10. "Why are we not valuing the word 'feminism'
when there is so much work to be done in terms
of empowerment and emancipation of women
everywhere?"
~ Annie Lennox

I will confess, on these pages, that I am a feminist—always have been. And a radical one at that—if radical means getting to and at the root of the problem.

I agree with Roxane Gay. I am also a Bad Feminist, in that I don't want to be seen as having all the answers, nor am I perfect, in any way.

At the same time, there is so much work to be done and we need to get on with it, not only in terms of empowering women but also in terms of saving the planet! Yes, I am one of those, too—an environmentalist, and an imperfect one at that.

Something for You to Consider: Do you have a set of values that are important to you? What are they?

||||||||||||||||||||||||||||||||||||||||||||||||||||||||||||||||||||||||||||||||||||||||||

11. "Magic in money. To me money can buy all kinds of things. Sure it can buy fancy things. But the real magic in money comes when people are starving and dying. Then money gives life and hope. It provides basics to survive. And for the rest of us, money magic conjures up a hot cup of tea or warm slippers in the winter or ice cream and a fan to cool us off in the summer. Or at any time a movie to make us laugh."
~ Karen Leeds

I kept this quote for the last because it says so much in such a simple yet eloquent way. I also wanted to leave you with your own thoughts since I've shared so many of my own, already, with more to come.

Something for You to Consider: What does this quote mean to you? What is precious and valuable? How is that reflected in your dreams?

41651260R00066

Made in the USA
Charleston, SC
07 May 2015